E
Bak     Baker, Eugene
        Safety first!  Fire

| DATE DUE | | | |
|---|---|---|---|
| OC 8 '92 | | | |
| MAR 02 | | | |
| APR 17 | | | |
| 10/20/95 | | | |
| FEB 05 | | | |
| JN 24 | | | |
| JL 30 | | | |
| NOV 01 97 | | | |
| MAY 04 | | | |
| JL 21 | | | |
| MY 17 '00 | | | |
| JE 28 01 | | | |

201-9500                         PRINTED IN U.S.A.

MEDIALOG
Alexandria, Ky 41001

# FIRE

By Eugene Baker
Pictures by Tom Dunnington

Zachary's Workshop LTD • Creative Education

Published by Creative Education, Inc.,
123 South Broad Street, Mankato, Minnesota 56001
Copyright ©1980 by Creative Education, Inc.
International copyrights reserved in all countries.
No part of this book may be reproduced in any form without
written permission from the publisher.
Printed in the United States.

Created by "Zachary's Workshop Ltd."
Lake Forest, Illinois 60045

Library of Congress Cataloging in Publication Data
Baker, Eugene H.
  Safety first . . . fire.
  SUMMARY: Illustrative episodes and safety
instructions highlight fire hazards at home, in
stores, and at campsites.
  1.  Fire prevention—Juvenile literature.
[1.  Fire prevention]  I.  Dunnington, Tom.
II.  Title
TH9148.B35     628.9'22     79-26636     ISBN 0-87191-735-1

Rover           Basil

"This place is spooky," said Basil. "Light some candles. Its time for our secret space monsters meeting."

"It's also a mess, Basil. I think we should clean up our club room."

Can you see what's wrong?

- Do not play with matches.
- Candles can be dangerous.
- Piles of rags and paper will burn by themselves.

"I smell smoke," said Rover. "What should we do?"

Basil sniffed the air. "Let's go see whats burning. Maybe Mom burned the beans again."

Can you see what's wrong?

- Have a fire drill plan in your home.
- Tell an adult you smell or see smoke.
- Get out at once—call for help.
- If smoke is in room—keep close to floor.

"Throw in that box," said Basil.
"It will burn fast."
"How many logs do we need?"
asked Rover. "Should I use this can?"

Can you see what's wrong?

13

- Have help when building a fire.
- Keep fire contained.
- Make sure fire is completely out before leaving room.
- NEVER spray lighter fluid on a fire.

"Look out! The pop corn oil is burning!" yelled Rover. "Turn off the burner."

"Should I throw some water on the pot?" shouted Basil. "The handle is hot!"

Can you see what's wrong?

17

- Keep a fire extinguisher in kitchen.
- Watch the stove when cooking.
- Be sure electric cord is in good repair.
- Do not overload an electrical outlet.
- Do not use the stove without an adult present.

19

"Look at the sparks," said Rover. "They go above the trees."

"That wood burns fast," laughed Basil. "The wind makes the fire jump really high!"

Can you see what's wrong?

21

- Do not get too close to a campfire.
- Use stones as a base at bottom.
- Be sure campfire is completely out before leaving.

23

"I see smoke," said Basil. "People are running."

"Wait! I want to buy this candy!" said Rover. "It is my favorite kind!"

Can you see what's wrong?

25

- Use a stairway or fire escape in a store—never an elevator.
- Look for the fire exit.
- Don't stop to look for friends or pets.
- Touch doors before opening— if hot, don't open.
- Walk—do NOT run.

27

# REMEMBER NOW. . . . . .

Do not play with matches.

Candles can be dangerous.

Piles of rags and paper will burn by themselves.

---

Have a fire drill plan in your home.

Tell an adult you smell or see smoke.

Get out at once—call for help.

If smoke is in room—keep close to floor.

Have help when building a fire.

Keep fire contained.

Make sure fire is completely out before leaving room.

NEVER spray lighter fluid on a fire.

---

Keep a fire extinguisher in kitchen.

Watch the stove when cooking.

Be sure electrical cord is in good repair.

Do not overload an electrical outlet.

Do not use the stove without an adult present.

Do not get too close to a campfire.

Use stones as a base at bottom.

Be sure campfire is completely out before leaving.

---

Use a stairway or fire escape in a store—never an elevator.

Look for the fire exit.

Don't stop to look for friends or pets.

Touch doors before opening— if hot, don't open.

Walk—do NOT run.

EUGENE BAKER is Vice-President for Curriculum and Materials Development, Zachary's Workshop Ltd., Lake Forest, Illinois. Dr. Baker graduated from Carthage College, Carthage, Illinois. He received his M.A. and Ph.D. in education from Northwestern University. He has worked as a teacher, as a principal, and as director of curriculum and instruction.

Gene is the author of many children's books, educational audio-visual materials, and numerous articles on reading, guidance, and learning research. One of his best-known series is the *I Want to Be* books. In addition to writing and speaking widely, he has served as consultant on various educational programs at both national and local levels. Dr. Baker also teaches Adult Sunday Church School.

Dr. Baker's practical help to schools where new programs are evolving is sparked by his boundless enthusiasm. He likes to see reading, social studies, and language arts taught with countless resources, including many books, to encourage students to think independently, creatively, and critically. Gene and his wife, Donna, live in Arlington Heights, Illinois. They have a son and two daughters.